S0-AYS-729

Created and published by Knock Knock
1635-B Electric Avenue
Venice, CA 90291
knockknockstuff.com

Illustrations by Gemma Correll

ISBN: 978-160106887-3
UPC: 825703-50099-8

10 9 8 7 6 5 4 3

100 Reasons to Panic® about Following Your Dreams

KNOCK
KNOCK®
VENICE, CALIFORNIA

1.

People will say you'd have a better chance finding a unicorn.*

You'll go broke.*

*Or you'll get rich. Filthy rich!

3.

You have no idea what you're getting yourself into.*

*Isn't that part of the appeal?

4.

Leaving your comfort zone is uncomfortable.*

*As long as you don't
go into the danger zone, you'll survive.

5.

Anything that can go wrong will go wrong.*

*Think of it as fodder for your future memoir!

6.

You're too
shy to network.*

<hr />

*Being shy just makes you more approachable.

7.

What will other people think?*

8.

Sayonara, Saturdays and Sundays!*

9.

You've got a fear of success.*

*Better that than a fear of failure.

10.

You've got a fear of failure.*

*Join the club.

11.

Friends will grow weary of being your cheerleader.*

*You'll be able return the favor someday.

12.

It's going to be hard.*

*Well, if it doesn't kill you, it will make you stronger-ish.

13.

If you quit
your job, you'll
lose security,
stability,
and a regular
paycheck.*

*You'll also lose that annoying coworker
who keeps swiping your stapler.

14.

People will think you're wasting your time.*

*You're taking the road less traveled.

15.

You'll have to do things that aren't your forte.*

*You're expanding your skill set.

16.

There aren't enough hours in the day to make it all happen.*

*You'll figure out how to survive on coffee and to-do lists.

17.

Plunging into the great unknown is scary.*

*It's your very own
choose-your-own-adventure novel!

18.

The odds aren't in your favor.*

*Lotteries aren't either—
but people win 'em all the time.

19.

Following your dreams will make your résumé look weird.*

*Or make it stand out
(just in case you need one again).

20.

You're not sure if it's the right time.*

*If you wait for the "right" time, you'll be waiting a looooong time.

21.

Some people seem to think you need a "real job."*

22.

Taking risks is, well, risky.*

*So is leaving the house.

23.

Your friends will secretly doubt you.*

*You'll make new friends who don't!

People will laugh at you.*

*You'll grow a thick skin, like a crocodile.

25.

You'll be going against the status quo.*

*You'll be challenging the status quo.

26.

You don't know what the heck you're doing.*

*You'll fall down. You'll get back up.

27.

You'll have to say no to dinner parties and other fun stuff.*

*No more stress about choosing an appropriately priced wine.

28.

You'll have to start from scratch.*

*Everybody has to start somewhere.

29.

More opportunities = more work.*

30.

Paperwork, taxes, legal crap? Yikes.*

*You'll get to refer to your accountant and your lawyer, which will make you sound fancy.

31.

You'll get around to your dream... someday.*

*The sooner you start, the sooner you can ignore all those other things on your to-do list.

32.

People will make assumptions about you.*

*You'll prove them wrong (or right).

- -

33.

With all the stress, you'll forget to eat.*

*Your grocery bills will plummet.

- -

34.

No one "gets" your dream.*

*You're cultivating an air of mystery.

35.

Your brain won't stop.*

*You'll be on the edge of your seat waiting for inspiration to strike. Exciting!

36.

Your stick-to-itiveness is a little intimidating.*

*Better to be feared than to be fearful.

37.

You'll come off as cocky.*

*Or you can wear your confidence like a very cool motorcycle jacket.

38.

Everyone will
want your advice
for following
their dreams.*

39.

what if your dreams are too big?*

*Setting smaller goals will be easy.

40.

What if your dreams are too small?*

*You'll get great practice at setting bigger goals.

41.

No one will want to buy your handmade dream catchers, candles, or mood rings.*

*You might be ahead
of the curve on the next Pet Rock.

You'll go into debt.*

*Most companies start out operating in the red.

43.

People will get tired of hearing about your project.*

*You'll be refining your elevator pitch.

44.

You'll be tempted to give up.*

*It'll make the payoff
that much sweeter when you don't.

45.

You feel like you're jumping off a cliff.*

*You'll grow wings! Or invest in a parachute . . .

46.

You'll get new wrinkles.*

Creme
de
Meh

*They add character.

47.

You'll have to hire help.*

*You'll have a small (but growing!) empire to rule.

48.

You don't have a mentor.*

*You can be someone else's
and create a legacy. Whoa.

49.

Someone will steal your good ideas.*

*What's that saying about imitation and flattery?

50.

You'll have to delegate.*

*You'll get to delegate.

51.

You have so many good ideas, it's hard to focus on just one.*

*If one doesn't work out, at least you have a plan B (or C, or D, or E).

52.

You'll start networking with anyone—or anything—who'll listen.*

*Who knows who—or what—you'll strike up a conversation with.

53.

Things might not go your way.*

*Or they'll be even more awesome than you dreamed.

54.

Sleepless nights will become the new normal.*

*So will power naps!

55.

You'll always be overbooked.*

*You can start charging for your appearances.

56.

No one else believes in your dream.*

*You're a visionary—
you've gotta believe in you first.

57.

Everyone else's life just seems so much more fun.*

*It probably is. (For now, anyway.)

58.

You'll have to do everything.*

*It'll make you understand every part of what you're doing better.

59.

Suddenly, you've developed a nervous twitch.*

*You're quirky!

60.

You'll lose perspective.*

*You'll gain insight.

61.

You'll need to spend a lot of time figuring a lot of stuff out.*

*It'll be like lifting weights—for your brain.

62.

You can't quit your day job yet.*

*Limited hours will force you
to be more efficient.

63.

You'll be plagued with self-doubt.*

*It'll add to your charm.

64.

You'll be forced to borrow money from annoying family members.*

*Hey, if they're willing to make you an interest-free loan, maybe they aren't so annoying.

65.

You'll have
to ask friends
for lots of favors,
then end up
alienating them.*

You're too young.*

*The early bird gets the worm.

67.

You're too old.*

*Better late than never.

68.

Your focus will make you a real bore at cocktail parties.*

*Or fellow partygoers will marvel at your drive and determination.

69.

You'll lose track of time.*

*Better that than watching the clock.

70.

You'll have to say "no" to a lot of stuff.*

*It'll make saying "yes" matter even more.

71.

Trusting your gut makes you a little uneasy.*

*You won't have to rely on psychics, tarot card readers, or fortune cookies.

72.

You've got so many dreams you'll need multiple lifetimes to follow them all.*

*If something doesn't come to fruition, onto the next!

73.

People will think you're nuts.*

*You'll be able to say "Told you so" when you're a huge success.

74.

You're still waiting for fame and fortune.*

*At least there aren't pesky paparazzi capturing you in sweats and sunglasses—yet!

75.

Some people will think it's time you throw in the towel.*

*Haters gonna hate.

76.

Your dream might change.*

*It's called growth and evolution.

77.

You'll have to burn the midnight oil.*

*You'll be nocturnal—just like honey badgers!

78.

You'll stop exercising and eating right.*

*And start wearing elastic-waist pants while eating cookies. Sounds pretty freeing, actually.

79.

You'll miss out on major life events.*

*You'll be the freewheeling friend.

80.

Your days will be packed to the gills.*

81.

Turns out your dream is expensive.*

*You'll figure out how to get creative on your taxes.

82.

You'll disappoint your parents.*

*Or make them weep with pride.

83.

You'll neglect your kid(s) and/or pet(s).*

*You're cultivating their independence.

84.

You won't have time for a relationship.*

*The last slice of pizza will always be yours.

85.

You'll neglect your relationship.*

*Your partner's golf game
will get really good.

You'll start spouting inspirational, self-helpy sayings.*

*You'll be everyone's go-to when they need a pep talk.

87.

You'll become certifiably obsessed.*

*Obsession is just another way
to say all-consuming passion.

88.

You'll get weird.*

*You're not weird, you're creative.

89.

You'll get bossy.*

*You're not bossy, you're empowered.

90.

You'll need to start meditating just to cope.*

*You can get a side gig as a spiritual guru. People pay big bucks for that.

91.

Your drive and passion could scare off potential dates.*

*Who needs dates? You've got drive and passion.

92.

You'll get way too into making a vision board.*

You'll have a real work of art
to hang above your sofa.

93.

You gotta
be you—even if
that means
letting your
freak flag fly.*

*If you don't, who else will?

94.

You feel out
of touch with
regular people
sometimes.*

*Regular people are overrated.

You'll kill
your plants.*

*You're not wasting water.

96.

You might hit a creative wall.*

97.

You'll get in over your head.*

*You'll get to figure out
if you're a sinker or a swimmer.

98.

The struggle is real.*

*So is the potential payoff.

99.

what if you're just not that good?*

100.

what if you fail?*

Don't worry.
It's worth it.